THE BROTHERS GRIMM

THE SEVEN RAVENS

ILLUSTRATED BY LISBETH ZWERGER

Translation from the German by Elizabeth D. Crawford

The copyright notice and Cataloging in Publication information are to be found on the last page.

WILLIAM MORROW AND COMPANY   NEW YORK   1981

A man had seven sons but no daughter, much as he longed for one. Finally his wife was expecting a child again, and when it came into the world, it was indeed a girl. Their joy was great, but the child was delicate and small, and because of her weakness she had to be baptized at once.

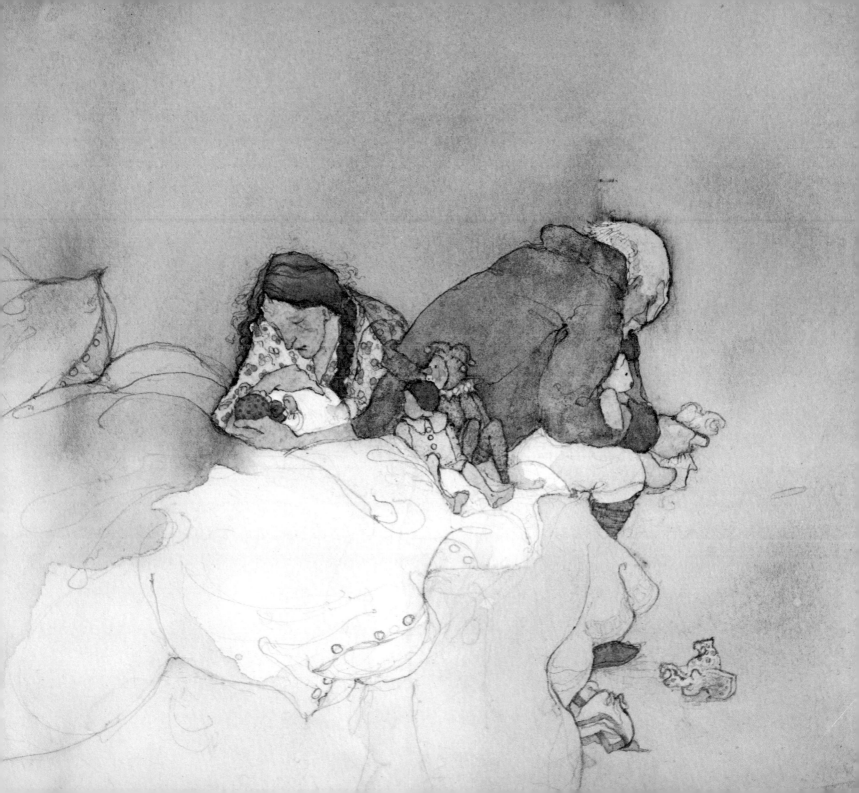

The father sent one of the boys hurrying to the well to fetch water for the baptism. The other six ran along with him, and while each one tried to be the first to draw the water, the pitcher fell into the well. They all stood there, not knowing what to do, and no one dared to go home.

When the boys did not come back, the father became impatient. "Have those young heathen stopped to play again and forgotten what I asked them to do?" he said. He grew anxious, lest the baby girl die unchristened, and in anger he cried, "I wish those boys would all turn to ravens!" Scarcely were the words out of his mouth when he heard a whirring in the air over his head and saw seven coal-black ravens fly up and away.

The parents could not unsay the
wish, and so, sorrowful as they were over the loss
of their seven sons, they nevertheless consoled
themselves in some measure with their dear little
daughter, who soon gained strength and became
more beautiful every day. For a long time, she did
not even know that she had any brothers, for her
parents took care not to mention them. Then one
day, by chance, the girl heard people talking
about her, saying that she was very beautiful, but
all the same she was to blame for the misfortune
of her seven brothers. She was cast down and
went to her father and mother and asked whether
she had indeed had brothers and where they had
gone. Now the parents could no longer keep the
secret, but they told her that what had befallen
them had been the decree of heaven and her birth
only the innocent occasion.

Every day, alone, the maiden pondered over what they had said and came to believe that she must set her brothers free. She had no rest or peace until she secretly got up and went out into the wide world to find her brothers and free them, wherever they were, cost what it would. She took nothing with her but a little ring as a memento of her parents, a loaf of bread for hunger, a little jug of water for thirst, and a little chair for weariness.

She walked and walked, far, far, to
the very ends of the earth. There she came to the
sun, but he was too hot and fearsome and he ate
little children. Quickly she fled and ran to the
moon, but the moon was too cold and hideous,
and she was cross, besides. When she saw the
maiden, she said, "Oh, ho, ho, I smell human
flesh." Then the maiden rushed away and came to

the stars, who were friendly and kind to her. Each sat in its very own little chair. But the morning star stood up and gave her a little bone and said, "Unless you have the little bone, you cannot open the glass mountain, and your brothers are there in this glass mountain."

The maiden took the little bone, wrapped it well in a kerchief, and went on again until she came to the glass mountain. The door was closed, and she went to take out the bone, but when she opened the kerchief, it was empty. She had lost the gift of the good star. What should she do? She wished to save her brothers and had no key to the glass mountain. The good little sister took a knife and cut off one of her fingers, stuck it in the door, and happily opened it. When she went in a dwarf came to meet her and said, "My child, what are you seeking?"

"I'm seeking my brothers, the seven ravens," she said.

The dwarf said, "The Masters Raven are not at home, but if you wish to wait here until they return, come in."

Then the dwarf brought in the ravens' food in seven little plates and seven little cups. From each plate the sister ate a small morsel, and from each cup she drank a sip; in the last cup she let fall the ring she had brought with her.

All at once there was a whirring and a crying in the air. "The Masters Raven are flying home now," said the dwarf.

They came, wished to eat and drink, and sought their plates and cups. Then said one after the other, "Who has eaten from my plate? Who has drunk from my cup? That was a human mouth."

And when the seventh came to the bottom of his cup, the little ring rolled against his mouth. Then he saw it and recognized that it was his parents' ring and said, "Would God that our own little sister were here, for then we should be free!"

When the maiden, who was standing behind the door listening, heard the wish, she came out, and then all the ravens regained their human forms again. And they embraced and kissed one another and went joyfully home.

Printed in the United States of America.
1   2   3   4   5   6   7   8   9   10

Library of Congress Cataloging in Publication Data

Grimm, Jakob Ludwig Karl, 1785-1863.
    The seven ravens.
Summary: A little girl walks to the end of the world to find her seven brothers
and free them from enchantment.
[1. Fairy tales. 2. Folklore—Germany]
I. Grimm, Wilhelm Karl, 1786-1859, joint author. II. Zwerger, Lisbeth. III. Title.
PZ8.G882Se   1981   398.2'1'0943   [E]   80-25365
ISBN 0-688-00371-0   ISBN 0-688-00372-9 (lib. bdg.)